The Beginning Of The Beginner

Learn Typing By Tutoring Yourself

The
Practical Way
To Learn
Practical Typing

Easy To Follow – All Laid Out For You

Dino Greco – Alex Greco – Marcia Tsuchiya – Tony Greco

The Beginning Of The Beginner

26 <u>Rhythmical</u> *Easy Typing Lessons for the Starting to Efficient Level Typist of Any Age*

This Method's concept is based exclusively on the use of 4 letter words organized into 26 lessons, each one having all of its words starting with one of the 26 alphabetic keys of the keyboard.

The 4 letter words concept is a smart approach to typing considering that around 65% of all commonly used words are made up of 4 letters or less.

The Beginning of the Beginner *is great for self teaching typing at any age and excellent in any learning setting*

ISBN: 1-4392-2471-4
ISBN-13: 9781439224717
Library of Congress Control Number: 2010907985

"The longer I practice,

the harder I practice,

the better I get."

\- Very Skillful Unknown Typist

Dedicated to Grandfather Domenico and Godmother Julia, we all are thinking of you everyday of our lives.

ALL OF THE INSTRUCTIONS WRITTEN IN THIS BOOK CAN BE HEARD IN ITS ENTIRETY ON THE AUDIO INSTRUCTIONS-PAGE OF THIS BOOK'S WEBSITE.

Visit this book's website at:

www.thebeginningofthebeginner.com

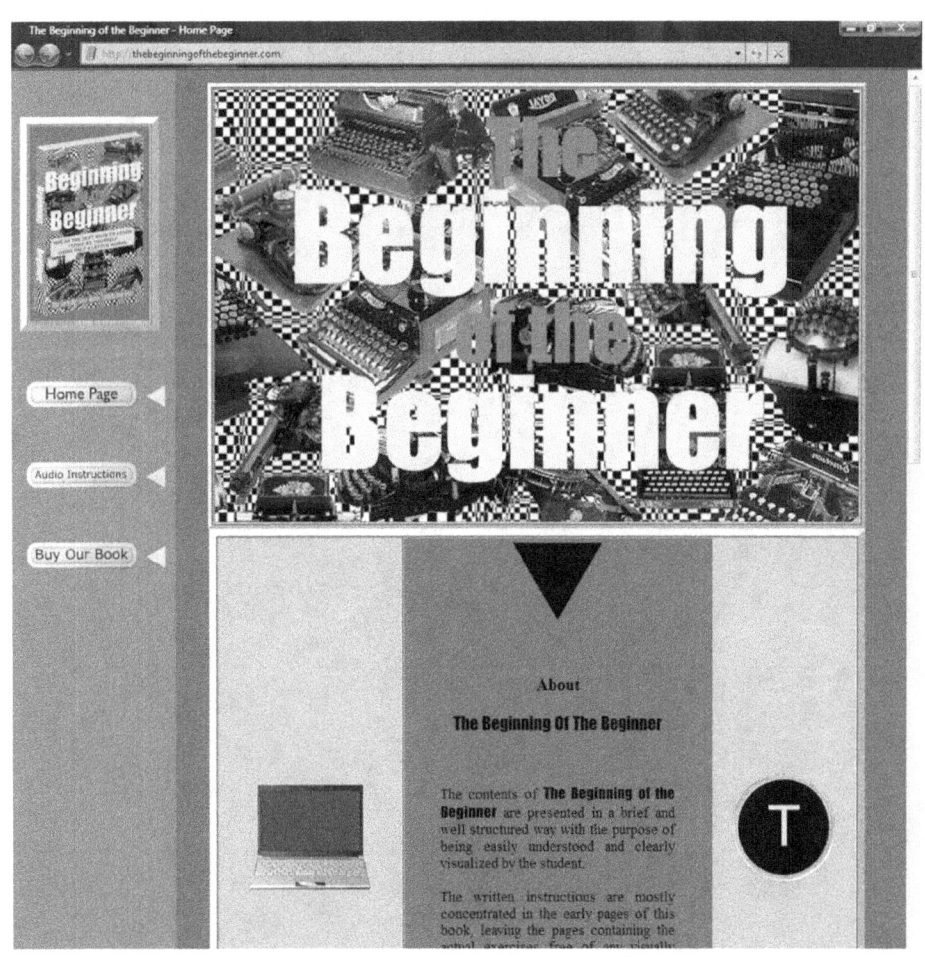

Contents

Presentation

The Beginning of the Beginner opens with an explanation of the original way in which this book is technically based on, along with the proper equipment setup and body posture in order to be comfortable while typing.

Soon after comes the introduction of the keyboard with the correct fingering to tap each key; then practical and technical typing tips and detailed instructions on how to practice the exercises in this book.

Next, the 3 main rows are introduced one at a time with their relative exercises. Once you have the knowledge of the position of the letters on the keyboard, the real practice on the words contained in the 26 lessons begins.

The 26 lessons contain the bulk of the exercises. The 1st, the 10th, and the 20th lessons include a few quick reminders of the general rules for correct practice which apply to all the lessons; these are nicely boxed and positioned on the right side of the pages.

The first 9 lessons focus on each of the 9 letters that make up the Home Row; followed by practice on complete sentences made with words picked from lessons 1 through 9; then a few exercises on the grammatical signs also located on the Home Row.

Lessons 10 to 19 focus on each of the 10 letters on the Top Row, followed by the same routine practice on sentences and grammatical signs also located on the Top Row.

The final lessons 20 through 26, which have the same characteristics of the previous 19 ones, are focused on the Bottom Row; they are followed by practice on complete sentences made by words contained in these lessons, and exercises on punctuation signs also located on the Bottom Row.

The book closes with an explanation of other signs and symbols on the keyboard; a table of roman numerals, and a brief creative illustrated history of the typewriter.

Concept

The concept of **The Beginning of the Beginner** is based on typing words beginning with one of the 26 alphabetic letters that are organized into 26 lessons according to the letter position on the keyboard.

In this innovative, advanced, modern typing book you will immediately start practicing on real, complete words, rather than go through months of practicing just on plain letters and signs, like with most of the traditional typing books.

This concept, obviously, is not a casual one but rather the result of a series of time consuming tests at the keyboard by the authors, which in many instances relied on feedback from beginner typing students about the way they would like a typing book to be structured in order for them to enjoy learning from it.

After several different practical tests in the search for the ultimate typing guide for beginner typists, finally the authors convened and consolidated **The Beginning of the Beginner**.

4 Letter Word Model

The **Four Letter Word Model** used in this method was established after counting several large samples of words taken randomly from the pages of a variety of books and magazines, then examining the statistical data collected. From this research the authors have found that on average about 55% to 65% of the words of any printed text are made up of 4 letter words or less; not taking into account the high number of five letter words used, which only exceeds four letter words by one letter.

To alleviate the beginner typist from the burden of practicing on text sources loaded with long, complicated words, the authors of this book have come-up with the **Four Letter Word Model**, a simple system yet a smart and effective one.

This model undoubtedly simplifies, for the beginner, the task involving the visual individuation of the location of each letter and sign on the keys of the keyboard. The reasoning is that short words also employ the frequent use of the space-bar, and a stroke of space-bar is a precious, convenient second in which to quickly regroup your concentration and reflexes, allowing time for your eyes to visually locate the next four letters on the keyboard and for your fingers to comfortably strike the four corresponding keys.

Typing Endurance

Typing Endurance at the keyboard is the gradual adapting process of the body and the mind to overcome the fatigue generated by the task of typing for hours at a time.

The authors of this book, as a means for reassurance, want you to know up-front that for the first few weeks of your typing practice, you will probably be able to endure this task for at most twenty minutes at a time; thereafter your patience would easily run out. If so, don't be concerned, that is the normal reaction expected from a beginner typist; *endurance* at the keyboard will come with time, practice, necessity and love for this task.

Accordingly, the authors conveniently arranged the timing practice of each lesson in this method to be within twenty minutes range. With time, the best way for you to start raising the bar of your *endurance* at the keyboard would be to practice the same lesson two or three times in the same session. Subsequently, you can further raise your *endurance* bar by typing down any interesting articles published in magazines or newspapers regarding any of your favorite subjects. Another useful great way to solidify your *endurance* is by neatly typing down your school's written assignments or by typing down the exact text of any letter you receive in your mailbox.

Endurance should be undoubtedly one of the main goals of the typist beside speed and spelling accuracy.

Your Setting at The Typing Station

- Free your workstation from any extra, loose, unorganized, distractive objects such as pens, pencils, erasers, notebooks, books, paper, etc.

- When using a standard keyboard, you can easily create an inclination by lifting the legs beneath it; however, if you are using a laptop on a table, do not just lay it flat, but rather use a laptop-stand to create the correct inclination which will ease the flexing of your fingers and wrists throughout all the typing they will be doing. Another benefit for using a laptop stand is that it elevates the laptop from the table creating airflow beneath it and reducing heat buildup in the laptop's components preventing them from overheating. (See figure 1)

Figure 1

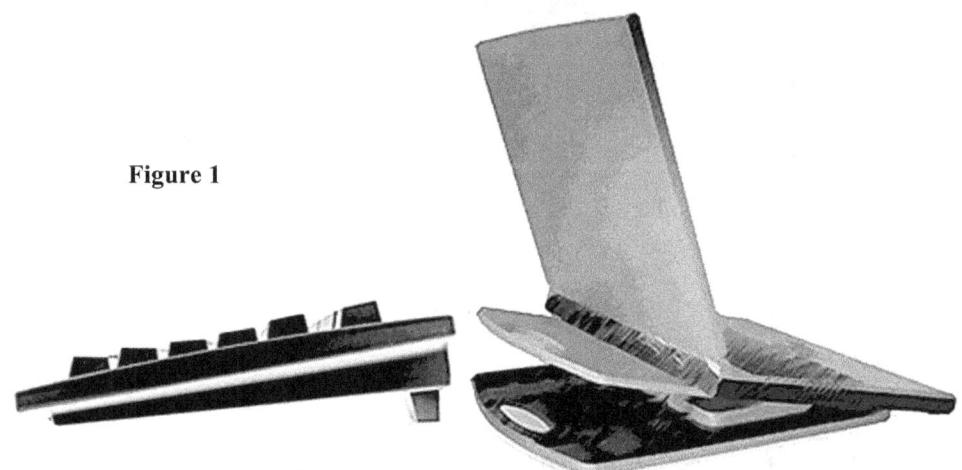

- For easy, comfortable reading-clarity, it is important to have good lighting illuminating the pages of this book or any other text on the stand, for this, a desk or floor gooseneck lamp pointed directly on the pages of the book will perfectly suit your needs. Avoid getting direct light in your eyes.

- When getting set for practice, place and adjust the stand with this book on it at a comfortable height in relation to your eyes, such that you don't have to bend your neck or back downward or upward in order to read from it. The best position to set this book, or any other text, is to place it on a **desk stand** on the left or right side of the monitor at an angle slightly slanted under the light of a **gooseneck lamp**. If on your worktable there is no room for a book rest or a lamp, simply use a **music stand** or something similar for your reading source and a **floor lamp** for lighting and you will be comfortably set. (See figure 2)

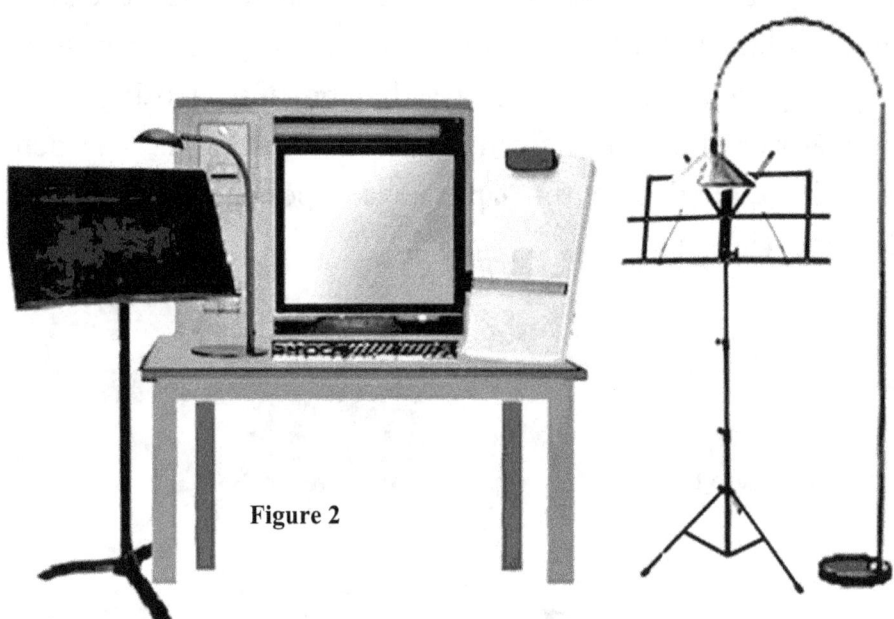

Figure 2

- When using a stand, you may sometimes need to fasten your text sources, the ones that are difficult to keep standing straight or fully open on it, such as a single soft sheet of paper, a newspaper page, a thick bulky book, an oversized brochure and so on. To prevent these from flying-away, folding-over, falling-off, or closing-up from the stand, you can use a variety of convenient little household gadgets such as paper clips, bag clips, elastic bands and other things of this nature. These handy gadgets are helpful in securing the texts sources on to the stand and keeping the page(s) of the text source(s) flat, avoiding annoying creases, bumps, crumples, or glare on the page making it much easier to read from. (See figure 3)

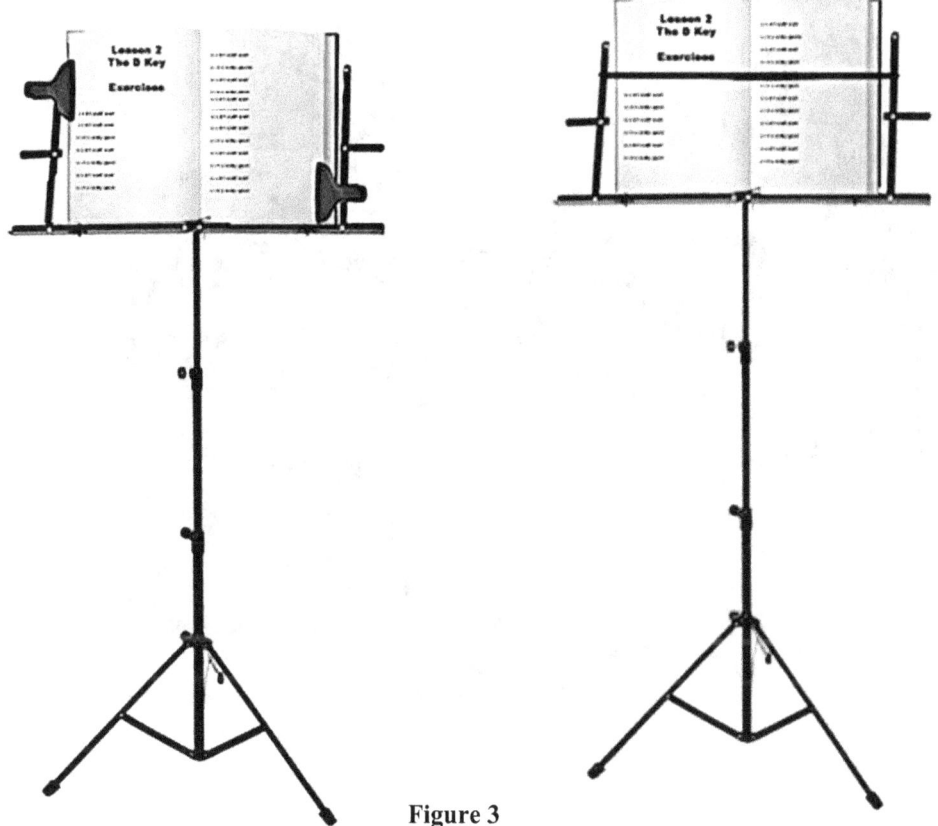

Figure 3

Typing Posture

Figure 4

- When sitting down at the workstation preparing for your daily typing practice, check that your posture is correct; for the correct typing posture refer to figure 4 above.

- For maximum, long-lasting sitting comfort, make sure that your back is upright and by any means pressed against the backrest of the chair.

You can hear the audio version of this page at www.thebeginningofthebeginner.com

- Be seated at a comfortable height and distance from the keyboard. (See figure 4 on page 8)

- Use the same type of low-back or mid-back chair as shown in figure 4 on page 8 and figure 5 on page 10.

- Adjust the height of the seat so your upper arms hang by your side with your elbows bent at 90° (see figure 4 on page 8).

- Adjust the backrest of your chair to give support to your lower back.

- Hold out your wrists in a straight neutral position not bent upward or downward.

- Keep your feet flat on the ground; utilize a footrest to place your feet if necessary.

The Eye-line

The Comfortable Eye-Line to Retain On the Monitor while Typing

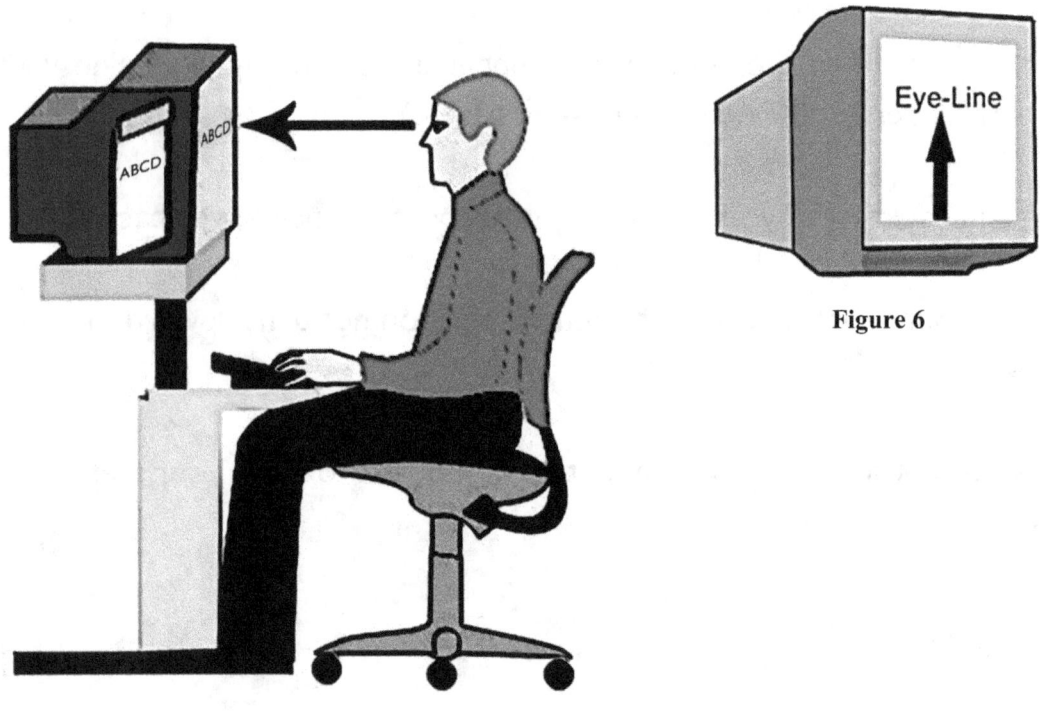

Figure 6

Figure 5

- Adjust the monitor so that your eyes are aligned with the top part of the screen, as shown in figures 5 and 6.

- Position the monitor about 2 feet away from your eyes.

- Use a stand to hold your text sources upright next to the monitor rather than laying them flat on the surface of the table you are working on.

While typing, for the comfort of your neck, back, and eyes, keep the ongoing typing line within the upper part of the screen. This can be achieved by periodically moving the already typed lines upward, you will manage to do so using the mouse, either by rolling its wheel or by using its pointer to move the scroll bar on the right side of the window you are working with.

The **Eye-Line** comfort height also applies to the text on the stand which you are reading and typing from. The text has to be at the same height as the screen, placed on a *tabletop stand* or a *floor stand* on the left or right side of the monitor. A way to have a truly mobile and efficient stand is to use a *music stand* which can easily be raised or lowered and moved to either side of the table or computer station.

The correct height of the **Eye-Line** in typing directly correlates with the upright comfort position of your neck and back, which is ultimately a determinant factor for a long and comfortable session of typing.

The Keyboard

Figure 7

 Used to indent a word

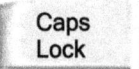 Used to make a letter UPPERCASE

 Used to delete any previous letter, sign or number

 Used to start new paragraphs and for vertical spacing

 Used to type the alternate upper characters on a key

 Used to space-out words, signs and numbers

You can hear the audio version of this page at www.thebeginningofthebeginner.com

Fingering

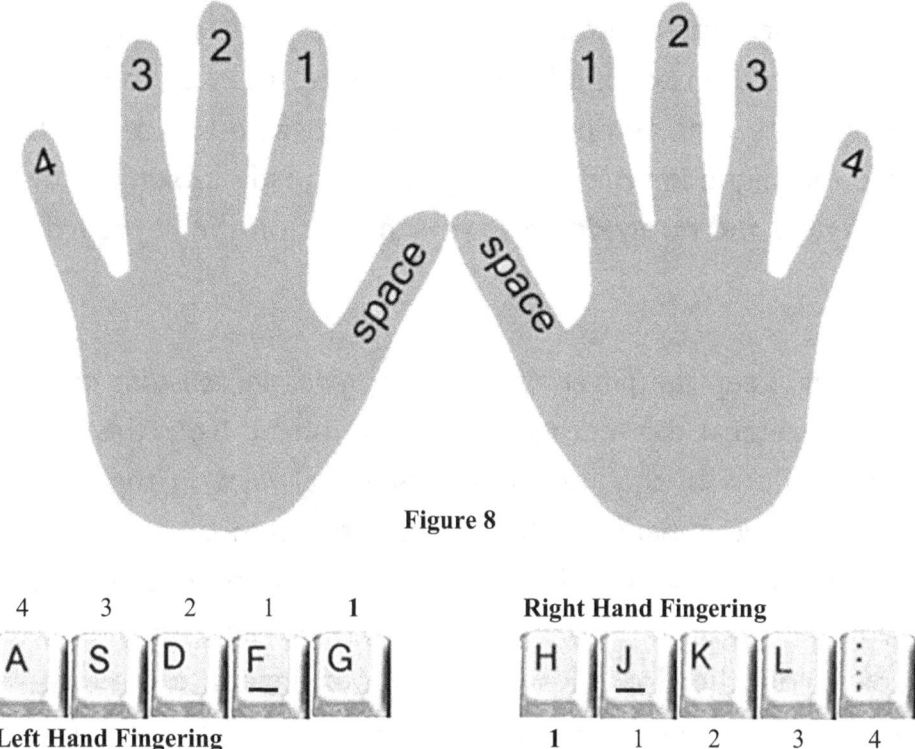

Figure 8

4	3	2	1	1
A	S	D	F	G

Left Hand Fingering

Right Hand Fingering

H	J	K	L	:
1	1	2	3	4

The ***little numbers above*** the letters, the signs, and the numbers, indicate the fingering for the keys to be punched with the **fingers of the *left* hand.**

The ***little numbers below*** the letters, the signs, and the numbers, indicate the fingering for the keys to be punched with the **fingers of the *right* hand.**

The **bold 1** above or below a letter, sign, or number indicates an extension of the left or right hand first fingers.

Most *Left handed* typists usually **space** with the left thumb.

Most *Right handed* typists usually **space** with the right thumb.

Thumbs are only used to type the space bar.

Tips for Good Typing

- In the beginning, practice the exercises in this book looking back and forth at the words in the text of a lesson and the position of your fingers on the keys. After, with time and practice you will be able to acquire *Touch-Typing* skills, the technique in which your eyes are mostly looking at the text that has been typed and rarely down at your fingers on the keyboard.

- When typing, *keep the finger tips of both hands in constant contact with the keys*: do not retreat the momentarily unused hand from the keyboard. The constant positions of the resting fingers are always on the Home Row. In order to keep your hands in the correct position on the keyboard make sure that the tip of the first finger of the left hand touches the bump on the **F** key and the tip of the first finger of the right hand touches the bump on the **J** key. From the Home Row extend your fingers to the lower or upper rows to type other letters and then return your fingers to the Home Row. The thumbs are always positioned on the space bar.

- It would be a very good practice technique to *speak-out* the name of words before typing them and the name of each letter of those words at the moment that you are typing them, such a task will add more solidity to your skills.

- When you are finished typing the words of a lesson, *clear the screen* by deleting all the words from that lesson. By doing so, you will always have a blank document which will give you a clear vision of what you are going to type next.

You can hear the audio version of this page at www.thebeginningofthebeginner.com

- For the first few weeks, practice the exercises making sure that your fingers *tap on the keys vigorously*. You'll need to gain strength in your fingers first: softness, agility and speed will follow later with time and practice.

- For maximum typing efficiency, make sure that when you start practicing, your hands are *warm* and *elastic*, if not that can be easily achieved by washing your hands with *warm water* and *soap*; also, when your hands are dry soften them by applying lotion.

Book View   # Monitor View

1 4

f a l l fall fall

 3 3

1   4 1

f l a g flag flag

  3

1 2 2 2

f e e d feed feed

1 1 2 2

f r e e free free

1 4 1 2

f a r e fare fare

This is the way that the exercises appear on the pages of this book.

F a l l fall fall

F l a g flag flag

F e e d feed feed

F r e e free free

F a r e fare fare

This is the way the words of the exercises will appear on your screen after you have typed them.

After getting settled at your typing station, prior to practicing the exercises in this book, you must first setup your word document to *print layout view* in order to get that particular dimensional sensation that you are typing a page on a traditional typewriter which allows you to see the text you are typing as if it was being typed on an actual sheet of paper.

In order to have a good view of the text that you are typing adjust the font size based on your screen resolution, for most settings a font **size of 20** is ideal.

Rhythm Vs. Rhythmical

Rhythm

Rhythm, in this book, is applied to the exercises in the 26 lessons as an agent of order, clarity, discipline and endurance meant to give a solid starting foundation to your typing. **Rhythm** is a work in progress, a temporary pattern exclusively applied to the exercises of the 26 lessons only.

*Read the extended **Rhythm** explanation on page 18.*

Rhythmical

Rhythmical, according to this book's teachings, should be the final stage of your typing technique. While the authors characterize Rhythm as a work in progress, they also regard **Rhythmical** typing as the final product. **Rhythmical** typing, as intended by the authors, is typing words in a more elastic pattern, freeing you from the constrained precise beat of rhythm.

*Read the extended **Rhythmical** explanation on page 19.*

You can listen to the practical audio demonstration of Rhythm versus Rhythmical on this book's website, www.thebeginningofthebeginner.com

Rhythm

Rhythm, per se, is the regular recurrence of movements in time. Many of the laws that regulate the structure and composition of the universe and life on Earth are influenced by **Rhythm**. In order to have an easy to practice, standard, solid pattern in all of the exercises in the 26 lessons, as a starting technical device, the **Rhythm** in this book is applied like music tempo, giving the typist the sensation of practicing a musical instrument. All the 26 lessons in this book are to be practiced with strict, precise **Rhythm** as explained on pages 20 and 21.

The set-up for the lessons in this book could simply be defined as a pattern of *typing by the second*, it consists of typing one letter per second, where each keystroke is equal to one second and a stroke of a space bar or a grammatical sign is also equal to a one second.

The aims of exercising using **Rhythm** in your typing are to gain security, solidity, strength, and speed in your fingers and in your mind. **Rhythm** will give a smooth upbeat continuity to your typing and make the initial approach to this task interesting, dynamic, and fun for all prospect typists of any age.

You can hear the audio version of this page at www.thebeginningofthebeginner.com

Rhythmical

Rhythmical, in the way that the authors of this book intended, is rhythm implemented with a reasonable degree of elasticity input into the precise cast of the metronome beat. The **Rhythmical** element is the motor that will keep your typing rolling steadily forward. The only exercises in this book that are to be typed using the **Rhythmical** speed are the exercises on the sentences made from words contained in the lessons, these sentences can be found on pages 58-60, 92 -94, and 119-121.

Rhythmical typing is based on the principle of typing the letters in a word with a continuous unbroken steady motion, making sure that you don't stop or pause while typing down the letters of a word. The only point where you stop or pause is on the punching of the spacebar that follows the word.

The **Rhythmical** speed is set by you, you will evaluate the typing speed you have acquired throughout your daily practice and gradually, time after time, you will adjust your **Rhythmical** speed to your degree of typing skill. In the beginning it is imperative to approach the typing of a text at a slow **Rhythmical** speed, always keeping your typing speed constant throughout that text at that time in that secession. In the next session, if you believe your technique has improved, retype that same text at a faster **Rhythmical** speed; again keeping your speed always constant throughout that session.

The pattern in which you are supposed to type is an unbroken ongoing non-stopping motion from the first letter of a word to the subsequent stroke of the space bar. Type in a non-stop even motion throughout all the letters in a word always up to the following spacebar which is the point of arrival and pause, then with the same motion start typing the letters of the next word up to the following spacebar stroke, which is again the point of arrival and pause.

Whenever there is any grammatical sign following a word, consider that sign as part of the non-stop **Rhythmical** pattern which will keep going until the following spacebar.
Keep practicing in this **Rhythmical** fashion and in a few weeks you will have gained a respectable typing ability which in the long term will progress into a more solid masterful typing technique.

Rhythmical typing is the essence of what the teaching of this book is all about; the unequivocal intent of the authors is to make you **type rhythmically** any document that you will ever tackle in your school setting, work place or personal matters.

Structure of the Exercises In the 26 Lessons

The typing pattern of most of the words in all the exercises in the 26 lessons is that each word must be typed with rhythm three times around.

The first time that the word is typed each of the letters are followed by a space, the second and third times the word is regularly typed without any spacing.

The easy pattern that the words are structured to be typed the first time around, in which each letter typed is followed by a stroke of the spacebar, allows you an extra moment to think about the position of the next key to be typed; the second and the third time around the word is typed normally since you have now acquired some familiarity about the location of the keys that correspond to the word.

The exercises are structured in this way in order to help you gradually transition from the beginning level of an insecure typist, constantly looking with your eyes down at the keyboard searching for the right key to be typed, to the advanced level of a *Touch-Typist* where you are looking primarily at the text sources.

Example :

1st TIME	2nd TIME	3rd TIME
f a l l	fall	fall

How to Practice the Exercises of the 26 Lessons in This Book

The initial time that you practice through the exercises of all the 26 lessons in this book, keep the speed of each stroke of a letter, a space, a punctuation sign or a number, constant at about one per second.

Each of the words in a lesson is typed with rhythm 3 times around; the typing pattern for each and every word in an exercise is always :

THE FIRST TIME

one letter | one space | *one letter* | one space | *one letter* | one space | *one letter* | one space |

THE SECOND TIME

letter letter letter letter | one space |

THE THIRD TIME

letter letter letter letter | one space |

You can hear the audio version of this page at www.thebeginningofthebeginner.com

Home Row

Left hand fingering

  4   3   2   1   1

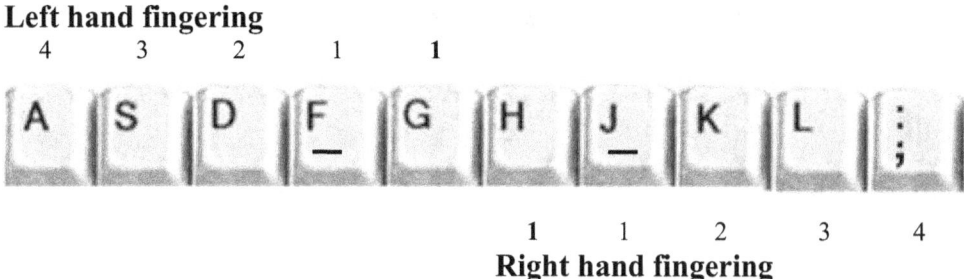

                       1   1   2   3   4

Right hand fingering

Home Row : Left Hand

– Exercises –

f f f f ffff ffff

d d d d dddd dddd

s s s s ssss ssss

a a a a aaaa aaaa

Home Row : Right Hand

– Exercises –

j j j j jjjj jjjj

k k k k kkkk kkkk

l l l l llll llll

; ; ; ; ;;;; ;;;;

Home Row : Left and Right Hand

– *Exercises* –

f j f j fjfj fjfj

d k d k dkdk dkdk

s l s l slsl slsl

a ; a ; a;a; a;a;

Home Row : Left and Right Hand
IST Finger the FG – JH Extensions

– Exercises –

g g g g gggg gggg

h h h h hhhh hhhh

f g f g fgfg fgfg

j h j h jhjh jhjh

Top Row

Left hand fingering
4   3   2   1   1

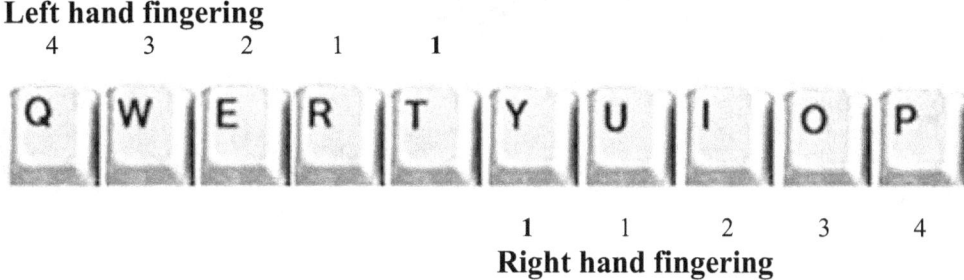

1   1   2   3   4
Right hand fingering

Top Row : Left Hand

— Exercises —

r r r r rrrr rrrr

e e e e eeee eeee

w w w w wwww wwww

q q q q qqqq qqqq

Top Row : Right Hand

— Exercises —

u u u u uuuu uuuu

i i i i iiii iiii

o o o o oooo oooo

p p p p pppp pppp

Top Row : Left and Right Hand

– Exercises –

r u r u ruru ruru

e i e i eiei eiei

w o w o wowo wowo

q p q p qpqp qpqp

Top Row : Left and Right Hand
1ST Finger the RT – UY Extensions

– Exercises –

t t t t tttt tttt

y y y y yyyy yyyy

r t r t rtrt rtrt

u y u y uyuy uyuy

Bottom Row

Left hand fingering

4   3   2   1   1

1   2   3   4

Right hand fingering

Bottom Row : Left Hand

– Exercises –

v v v v vvvv vvvv

c c c c cccc cccc

x x x x xxxx xxxx

z z z z zzzz zzzz

Bottom Row : Right Hand

– Exercises –

n n n n nnnn nnnn

m m m m mmmm mmmm

, , , , ,,,, ,,,,

. . . .

Bottom Row : Left and Right Hand

– Exercises –

v n v n vnvn vnvn

c m c m cmcm cmcm

x , x , x,x, x,x,

z . z . z.z. z.z.

Bottom Row : Left Hand
1ST Finger the VB Extension

– Exercises –

b b b b bbbb bbbb

v b v b vbvb vbvb

Number Row

Left Hand Fingering

4   3   2   1   **1**

1   1   2   3   4

Right Hand Fingering

Number Row : Left Hand

– Exercises –

4 4 4 4 4444 4444

3 3 3 3 3333 3333

2 2 2 2 2222 2222

1 1 1 1 1 1111 1111

Number Row : Right Hand

– Exercises –

7 7 7 7 7777 7777

8 8 8 8 8888 8888

9 9 9 9 9999 9999

0 0 0 0 0 0000 0000

Number Row : Left and Right Hand

– Exercises –

4 7 4 7 4747 4747

3 8 3 8 3838 3838

2 9 2 9 2929 2929

1 0 1 0 1010 1010

Number Row : Left and Right Hand
1ST Finger the 4,5 – 7,6 Extensions

– Exercises –

5 5 5 5 5555 5555

6 6 6 6 6666 6666

4 5 4 5 4545 4545

7 6 7 6 7676 7676

LESSON 1

– THE F KEY –

– *Exercises* –
Practice with Rhythm

Instructions for All the Exercises

^{1 4}
f a l l fall fall
_{3 3}

Pattern of the Exercises
Letter space *letter* space *letter* space *letter* space
Letter letter letter letter space *letter letter letter letter* space
Hit the **Enter** key after each line of words

^{1 4 1}
f l a g flag flag
₃

The exercises are to be typed in **lowercase** font **size 20** on a page set-up in **print layout view**.

^{1 2 2 2}
f e e d feed feed

When typing the word the **first** time, which is spaced-out, look down at the keyboard to memorize the keys; when typing it regularly the **second** and **third** time, look up at screen to check its spelling.

^{1 1 2 2}
f r e e free free

Before typing each word, say it aloud once, and then type it down three times

^{1 4 1 2}
f a r e fare fare

After typing 7 or 8 lines of words scroll the page up to keep a comfortable eye-line

^{1 4 2 2}
f a d e fade fade

^{1 2 2}
f e e l feel feel
₃

^{1 2 2 **1**}
f e e t feet feet

¹
f i l l fill fill
_{2 3 3}

¹
f o o l fool fool
_{3 3 3}

¹
f l o p flop flop
_{3 3 4}

¹
f u l l full full
_{1 3 3}

^{1 2}
f e l l fell fell
_{3 3}

^{1 2}
f o o d food food
_{4 4}

*The numbers **above** the letters indicate the use of the fingers of the **left hand**.*
*The numbers **below** the letters indicate the use of the fingers of the **right hand**.*
*Bold **1**'s indicate the extension of the 1st fingers.*

*The constant position of the resting fingers are always on the Home Row, the tip of the first finger of the left hand touches the <u>bump</u> on the **F** key and the tip of the first finger of the right hand touches the <u>bump</u> on the **J** key. From the Home Row extend your fingers to the lower or upper rows to type other letters and then return your fingers to the Home Row.*
The thumbs are always positioned on the space bar.

1   1
f o o t foot foot
3   3

1   2 2
f l e e flee flee
3

1   3 3
f u s s fuss fuss
1

1   2 3
f l e w flew flew
3

1   4 3
f l a x flax flax
3

1   4
f l a n flan flan
3   1

Re-type each lesson a few times around

After typing the last word of a lesson, completely clear
the pages on the screen for the next round of practice

Apply all of the boxed instructions above to all of the 26 lessons

33

LESSON 2

– THE D KEY –

– *Exercises* –

Practice with Rhythm

2   4   3
d a s h dash dash
1

2   2   2   2
d e e d deed deed

2   2   2
d e e p deep deep
4

2
d u l l dull dull
1   3   3

2
d i l l dill dill
2   3   3

2
d o l l doll doll
3   3   3

d e l l dell dell

d o o r door door

d a d o dado dado

d u d e dude dude

d o d o dodo dodo

d i d o dido dido

d e a f deaf deaf

d e a r dear dear

2 4 1 1
d a r t dart dart

2 2 3
d e s k desk desk
2

2 4 1
d a r k dark dark
2

2 2 4
d e a l deal deal
3

2 4
d a n k dank dank
1 2

2 1 2
d i r e dire dire
2

LESSON 3

– *Exercises* –

Practice with Rhythm

3 4 3 3
s a s s sass sass

3 4 3
s a s h sash sash
1

3   4 1
s l a g slag slag
3

3 2 2 2
s e e d seed seed

3 2 2
s e e k seek seek
2

3 2 2
s e e p seep seep
4

37

³
s i l l sill sill
_{2 3 3}

³
s h o o shoo shoo
_{1 3 3}

^{3 2}
s e l l sell sell
_{3 3}

^{3   1}
s o o t soot soot
_{3 3}

_{3 4   3 3}
s a w s saws saws

_{3 4   1 2}
s a f e safe safe

_{3 2 4 1}
s e a r sear sear

_{3 4 2}
s a c k sack sack
₂

38

3

s o i l soil soil
3 2 3

3

s o l o solo solo
3 3 3

3

s o u l soul soul
3 1 3

3

s i l o silo silo
2 3 3

3 4   3

s a n s sans sans
1

3 4   1

s a n g sang sang
1

LESSON 4

– *Exercises* –

Practice with Rhythm

4 2 2 3
a d d s adds adds

4 4 3
a l a s alas alas
  3

4 1 4 1
a f a r afar afar

4 **1** 4 1
a g a r agar agar

4 3 4
a w a y away away
  1

4 3 1
a w r y awry awry
  1

40

4

a l l y ally ally

3 3 1

4 1

a t o p atop atop

3 4

4 4 4

a q u a aqua aqua

1

4 1 2

a g u e ague ague

1

4 1 1

a g o g agog agog

3

4 2 3

a p e s apes apes

4

4 3 2

a p s e apse apse

4

4 2 2

a i d e aide aide

2

⁴   ⁴ ¹

a j a r ajar ajar
₁

⁴   ²

a l o e aloe aloe
₃ ₃

⁴   ³

a l m s alms alms
₃ ₂

⁴ ¹

a l t o alto alto
₃ ₃

⁴ ¹

a u t o auto auto
₁ ₃

LESSON 5

– THE $\boxed{\text{G}}$ KEY – Left hand 1st finger extension

– *Exercises* –
Practice with Rhythm

1 4 1 1

g a f f gaff gaff

1 4 2 3

g a d s gads gads

1 4 3

g a s h gash gash
    1

1 4

g a l l gall gall
  3 3

1 4 3

g a l s gals gals
  3

1 4 4

g a l a gala gala
  3

1   4 2

g l a d glad glad

  3

1 4 1 2

g a g e gage gage

1 2 4 1

g e a r gear gear

1 1 4 2

g r a d grad grad

1 1 2 3

g r e w grew grew

1 2 2

g e e k geek geek

    2

1

g i l l gill gill

 2 3 3

1 4 2

g a l e gale gale

  3

1 1   1

g r o g grog grog

₃

1   4   1

g a n g gang gang

₁

1   4 2

g o a d goad goad

₃

1   2 2

g l e e glee glee

₃

1   2

g o o d good good

_{3   3}

1   1

g o o f goof goof

_{3   3}

LESSON 6

– THE J KEY –

– *Exercises* –

Practice with Rhythm

⁴ ¹ ³
j a g s jags jags
¹

j u l y july july
¹ ¹ ³ ¹

²
j u k e juke juke
¹ ¹ ²

⁴ ¹ ³
j a r s jars jars
¹

⁴ ³ ³
j a w s jaws jaws
¹

⁴ ² ²
j a d e jade jade
¹

j e e r jeer jeer

j e s t jest jest

j i l t jilt jilt

j o s h josh josh

j o w l jowl jowl

j a i l jail jail

j e l l jell jell

j e e p jeep jeep

j e r k jerk jerk

j a p e jape jape

j a v a java java

j a z z jazz jazz

j a c k jack jack

j a m b jamb jamb

LESSON 7

– *Exercises* –

Practice with Rhythm

k o o k kook kook
2 3 3 2

4 1 1
k a r t kart kart
2

2 3
k i d s kids kids
2 2

3 3
k i s s kiss kiss
2 2

1 3
k i t s kits kits
2 2

1 2
k i t e kite kite
2 2

k i t h kith kith

    1
2 2   1

k e l p kelp kelp

    2
2 3 4

k e e p keep keep

  2 2
2   4

k e e l keel keel

  2 2
2   3

k a l e kale kale

  4 2
2   3

k e p t kept kept

  2   1
2   4

k e y s keys keys

  2   3
2   1

k h a n khan khan

    4
2 1   1

50

k i l n kiln kiln
2 2 3 1

k i n k kink kink
2 2 1 2

k n o w know know
     3
2 1 3

k n e e knee knee
  2 2
2 1

k i c k kick kick
    2
2 2 2

k e e n keen keen
  2 2
2 1

51

LESSON 8

– THE $\boxed{\text{L}}$ KEY –

– *Exercises* –

Practice with Rhythm

4 2 3
l a d s lads lads
3

4 3 3
l a s s lass lass
3

4 1 3
l a g s lags lags
3

4 3
l a s h lash lash
3   1

l u l l lull lull
3 1 3 3

l o l l loll loll
3 3 3 3

l o o k look look
3 3 3 2

l o o p loop loop
3 3 3 4

l o o t loot loot
3 3 3 1

2 2 1
l e e r leer leer
3

2 3 3
l e s s less less
3

2 2 3
l e e s lees lees
3

3 3
l o s s loss loss
3 3

2 2
l e e k leek leek
3   2

53

l u l u lulu lulu
3 1 3 1

4 1 4
l a v a lava lava
3

4
l a n k lank lank
3 1 2

4 2
l a c k lack lack
3 2

4 2
l a n d land land
3 1

4 1
l a m b lamb lamb
3 2

54

LESSON 9

– THE $\boxed{\text{H}}$ KEY – Right hand 1ˢᵗ finger extension

– *Exercises* –

Practice with Rhythm

⁴
h a l l hall hall
₁ ₃ ₃

⁴ ¹
h a l f half half
₁ ₃

h o o k hook hook
₁ ₃ ₃ ₂

h o o p hoop hoop
₁ ₃ ₃ ₄

h u l l hull hull
₁ ₁ ₃ ₃

h i l l hill hill
₁ ₂ ₃ ₃

h o o d hood hood
2
1 3 3

h o o f hoof hoof
1
1 3 3

h o o t hoot hoot
1
1 3 3

h a d e hade hade
4 2 2
1

h a r d hard hard
4 1 2
1

h a r e hare hare
4 1 2
1

h e r e here here
2 1 2
1

h e r s hers hers
2 1 3
1

h e e l heel heel
2 2
1   3

h a n k hank hank
4
1   1 2

h a c k hack hack
4 2
1   2

h a m s hams hams
4   3
1   2

h a n d hand hand
4   2
1   1

h a n g hang hang
4   1
1   1

Sentences made from Words of Lessons 1-9

– Exercises –

Practice Rhythmically

The gals won a sash.

> First read each sentence aloud, and then **rhythmically** type it down once using a period at the end.

Half the lads were glad.

Alas the lass lost a sash.

Half of the lads were glad.

The gals will fall in the hall.

The gals and lads were glad.

The lass will dash to the gala.

Half the flag will fall in the hall.

Alas the lass will fall in the hall.

The lass got a sash for the dash.

The lads had to dash in the hall.

The lass wore a sash at the gala.

Half the flag will lash in the wind.

The lads made a dash in the hall.

The lads made jags with the gads.

The lass had the gall to show sass.

The gals are glad to be at the gala.

The lads had a gash from the lash.

The lads got a gash from the gads.

The lads and gals went to the gala.

Exercises on the 4 punctuation signs located on the Home Row

Semicolon	;
Colon	:
Apostrophe	'
Quotes	" "

Exercises on the Semicolon ;

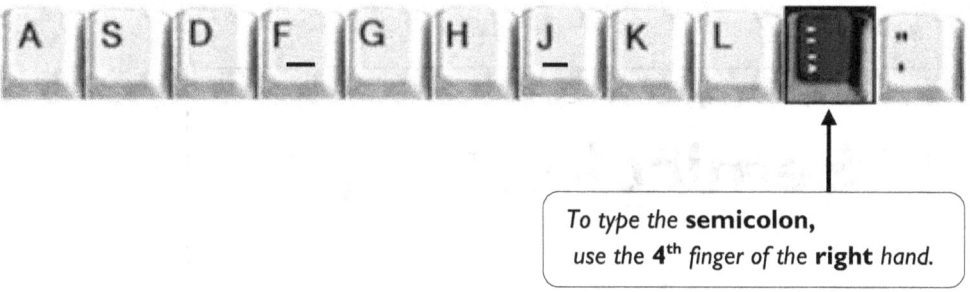

To type the **semicolon,**
use the **4th** finger of the **right** hand.

– *Exercises* –

Practice with Rhythm

flag; flag;

alas; alas;

gads; gads;

glad; glad;

jags; jags;

lads; lads;

half; half;

Exercises on the Colon :

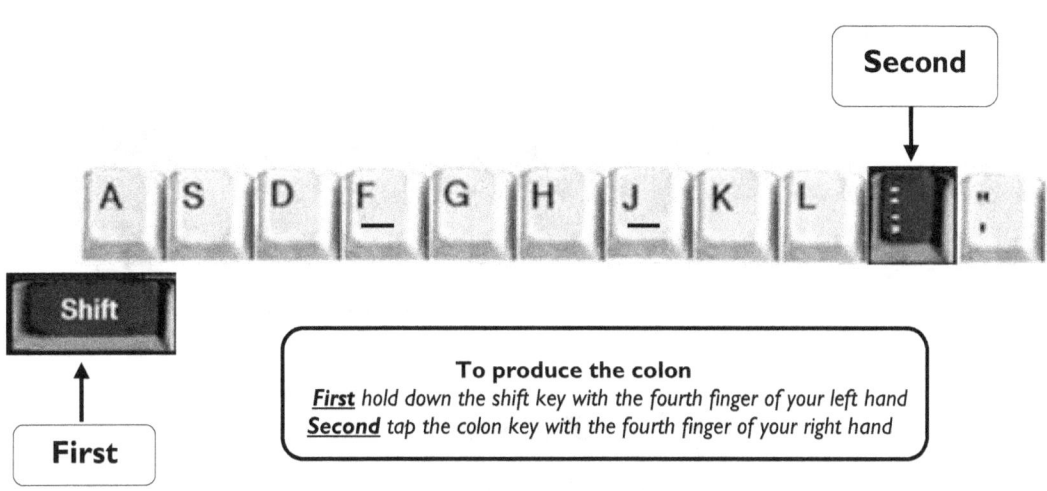

Second

First

Shift

To produce the colon
First hold down the shift key with the fourth finger of your left hand
Second tap the colon key with the fourth finger of your right hand

– *Exercises* –
Practice with Rhythm

fall: fall:

sass: sass:

adds: adds:

gaff: gaff:

Pattern of the keys
Type the word – hold down the shift key – tap the colon key – space.
*Repeat this pattern two times for each word then hit the **enter** key.*

gall: gall:

lass: lass:

hall: hall:

Exercises on the Apostrophe '

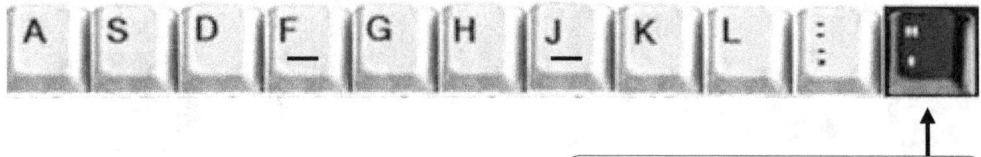

To type the **apostrophe,**
use the **4th** finger of the **right** hand.

– *Exercises* –

Practice with Rhythm

flag' flag'

alas' alas'

gads' gads'

glad' glad'

jags' jags'

lads' lads'

lags' lags'

Exercises on the Quotes " "

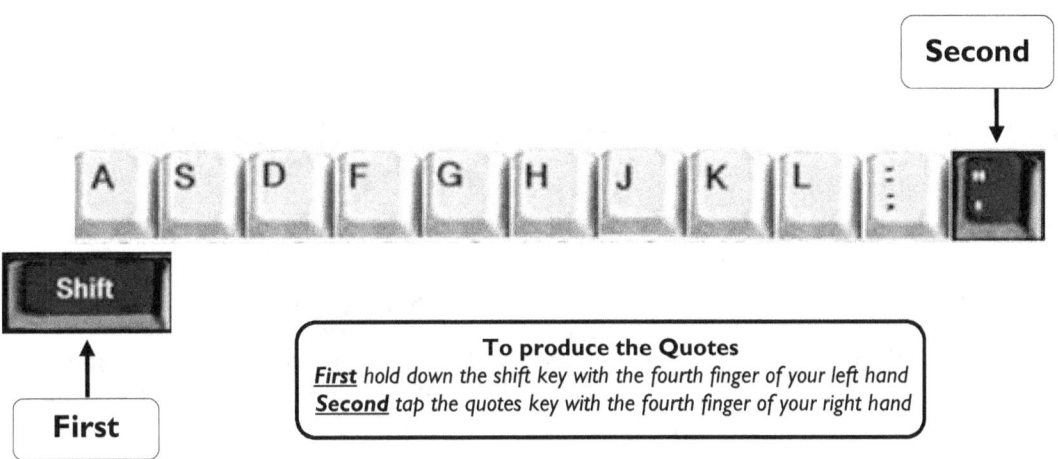

Second

A S D F G H J K L : "

Shift

First

To produce the Quotes
First hold down the shift key with the fourth finger of your left hand
Second tap the quotes key with the fourth finger of your right hand

– Exercises –

Practice with Rhythm

"fall fall"

"sass sass"

"adds adds"

"gaff gaff"

"gall gall"

"lass lass"

"hall hall"

Pattern of the keys
Hold down the shift key – tap the quotes key – Type the word twice
– hold down the shift key again – tap the quotes key again – space.
*Repeat this pattern for each word then hit the **enter** key.*

LESSON 10

– THE R KEY –

– *Exercises* –

Practice with Rhythm

Instructions for All the Exercises

1 2
r e p o repo repo
    4 3

Pattern of the Exercises
Letter space *letter* space *letter* space *letter* space
Letter letter letter letter space *letter letter letter letter* space
Hit the **Enter** key after each line of words

1   2
r i p e ripe ripe
 2 4

The exercises are to be typed in **lowercase** font **size 20** on a page set-up in **print layout view**.

1   2
r o p e rope rope
 3 4

When typing the word the **first** time, which is spaced-out, look down at the keyboard to memorize the keys; when typing it regularly the **second** and **third** time, look up at screen to check its spelling.

1   1
r o u t rout rout
 3 1

1   1
r i o t riot riot
 2 3

Before typing each word, say it aloud once, and then type it down three times

1   1
r o o t root root
 3 3

After typing 7 or 8 lines of words scroll the page up to keep a comfortable eye-line

66

1 **1** 2
r i t e rite rite
  2

1 2 2 2
r e e d reed reed

1 2   2 1
r e e f reef reef

1 2 2
r e e k reek reek
  2

1 2   2
r e e l reel reel
   3

1
r o o k rook rook
  3   3   2

1
r o l l roll roll
  3 3 3

1   1
r o o f roof roof
  3   3

> The numbers **above** the letters indicate the use of the fingers of the **left hand**.
> The numbers **below** the letters indicate the use of the fingers of the **right hand**.
> Bold **1**'s indicate the extension of the 1ˢᵗ fingers.

> The constant position of the resting fingers are always on the Home Row, the tip of the first finger of the left hand touches the _bump_ on the **F** key and the tip of the first finger of the right hand touches the _bump_ on the **J** key. From the Home Row extend your fingers to the lower or upper rows to type other letters and then return your fingers to the Home Row.
> The thumbs are always positioned on the space bar.

¹   ²
r o o d rood rood
³ ³

¹   ¹ ¹
r i f f riff riff
²

¹
r i l l rill rill
² ³ ³

¹   ¹ ¹
r u f f ruff ruff
¹

¹ ⁴ ¹ ²
r a r e rare rare

¹ ²   ⁴ ¹
r e a r rear rear

> *Re-type each lesson a few times around*

> *After typing the last word of a lesson, completely clear
> the pages on the screen for the next round of practice*

> **Apply all of the boxed instructions above to all of the 26 lessons**

LESSON 11

– THE E KEY –

– *Exercises* –

Practice with Rhythm

² ¹
e t u i etui etui
₁ ₂

² ¹
e u r o euro euro
₁ ₃

² ¹ ¹ ³
e g g s eggs eggs

² ² ³
e e l s eels eels
₃

² ² ²
e d d y eddy eddy
₁

² ⁴ ³ ²
e a s e ease ease

2 3 2
e l s e else else
3

2 2 3
e y e s eyes eyes
1

2 4 1 3
e a r s ears ears

2 1 4 3
e r a s eras eras

2 4 3 1
e a s t east east

2 2 1 2
e d g e edge edge

2 4 1 3
e a t s eats eats

2 1 4 2
e g a d egad egad

2 4 3
e a s y easy easy
1

2 1 1
e r g o ergo ergo
3

2 2 1
e d i t edit edit
2

2 3
e s p y espy espy
4 1

2 1 3
e g o s egos egos
3

2 3
e l k s elks elks
3 2

LESSON 12

– *Exercises* –

Practice with Rhythm

3 2 2
w e e p weep weep
4

3   2 1 2
w e r e were were

3   2 1 **1**
w e r t wert wert

3 2   1
w e i r weir weir
2

3 2   **1**
w e p t wept wept
4

3   1 2
w i r e wire wire
2

72

3   1 2
w o r e wore wore
  3

3 2 2 2
w e e d weed weed

3 4 1 1
w a t t watt watt

3 2 2
w e e k week week
  2

3
w o o l wool wool
  3 3 3

3
w i l l will will
  2 2 3

3 4
w a l l wall wall
  3 3

3 2
w e l l well well
  3 3

3   1
w o o f woof woof
 3   3

3   2
w o o d wood wood
 3   3

3   2 3
w h e w whew whew
 1

3   4 2 2
w a d e wade wade

3   4 1 2
w a r d ward ward

3   4 1 1
w a f t waft waft

LESSON 13

– THE Q KEY –

– Exercises –

Practice with Rhythm

4
q u i p quip quip
1 2 4

4   1
q u i t quit quit
1 2

4   2
q u i d quid quid
1 2

4 1 4 2
q u a d quad quad

4   4
q u a y quay quay
1   1

LESSON 14

– THE $\boxed{\text{T}}$ KEY – Left hand 1ˢᵗ finger extension

– *Exercises* –

Practice with Rhythm

1 1 2 2
t r e e tree tree

1   1
t o o t toot toot
　3　3

1   1
t u t u tutu tutu
　1   1

1
t y p o typo typo
1   4   3

1 1
t r o y troy troy
　3　1

1 1   2
t r u e true true
　1

1 1   1
t r o t trot trot
3

1 3   1
t w i t twit twit
2

1   1
t o u r tour tour
3 1

1   1
t o u t tout tout
3 1

1   2
t y p e type type
1 4

1   1 1
t o r t tort tort
3

1   1 1
t o r t tort tort
3

1 2 2 2
t e e d teed teed

1 2 2 3
t e e s tees tees

1
t i l l till till
 2 3 3

1
t o o l tool tool
 3 3 3

1
t o o k took took
 3 3 2

1 4
t a l l tall tall
 3 3

1 2
t e l l tell tell
 3 3

LESSON 15

– *Exercises* –

Practice with Rhythm

3 2 3
u s e s uses uses
1

u p o n upon upon
1 4 3 1

3
u m p s umps umps
1 2 4

1
u n i t unit unit
1 1 2

4
u l n a ulna ulna
1 3 1

3 2 2
u s e d used used
1

3 2 1

u s e r user user
1

1 2 4

u r e a urea urea
1

1 **1** 2

u r g e urge urge
1

2

u n d o undo undo
1 1   3

1

u n t o unto unto
1 1   3

1   2

u r i c uric uric
1   2

1   3

u r n s urns urns
1   1

4   3

u z i s uzis uzis
1   2

80

LESSON 16

– THE $\boxed{\text{I}}$ KEY –

– Exercises –

Practice with Rhythm

³
i l l s ills ills
_{2 3 3}

^{1 1}
i f f y iffy iffy
_{2 1}

^{1 3}
i r i s iris iris
_{2 2}

^{3 3}
i w i s iwis iwis
_{2 2}

^{1 3}
i b i s ibis ibis
_{2 2}

^{2 2 4}
i d e a idea idea
₂

i[2] d e[2] s[3] ides ides
[2]

i d[2] l e[2] idle idle
[2] [3]

i l[2] e a[4] ilea ilea
[2] [3]

i l[2] e x[3] ilex ilex
[2] [3]

i o[1] t a[4] iota iota
[2] [3]

i d o[2] l idol idol
[2] [3] [3]

i d l[2] y idly idly
[2] [3] [1]

i r[1] k s[3] irks irks
[2] [2]

82

LESSON 17

– *Exercises* –

Practice with Rhythm

       4

o l l a olla olla

3 3 3

        3

o o p s oops oops

3 3 4

     2 2 3

o d d s odds odds

3

    1 1 3

o f f s offs offs

3

    1 2 2

o g e e ogee ogee

3

o l i o olio olio

3 3 2 3

o l e o oleo oleo
2
3 3 3

o d o r odor odor
2 1
3 3

o p u s opus opus
3
3 4 1

o i l s oils oils
3
3 2 3

o w e d owed owed
3 2 2
3

o d e s odes odes
2 2 3
3

o a r s oars oars
4 1 3
3

o w e s owes owes
3 2 3
3

84

o a f s oafs oafs
4 1 3
3

o l d s olds olds
2 3
3 3

o p a l opal opal
4
3 4 3

o k a y okay okay
4
3 2 1

o a t h oath oath
4 1
3 1

o a k s oaks oaks
4 3
3 2

LESSON 18

– THE $\boxed{\text{P}}$ KEY –

– *Exercises* –

Practice with Rhythm

p o o p poop poop
4 3 3 4

          1
p o o r poor poor
4 3 3

     1 1
p u t t putt putt
4 1

     1 1
p u f f puff puff
4 1

     2
p o p e pope pope
4 3 4

     2
p i p e pipe pipe
4 2 4

86

p e e r peer peer
4

p e r t pert pert
4

p r e p prep prep
4

p o o l pool pool
4 3 3 3

p i l l pill pill
4 2 3 3

p o o f poof poof
4 3 3

p a s s pass pass
4

p e e k peek peek
4

p e e l peel peel
^{2 2}
_{4   3}

p a l l pall pall
⁴
_{4   3 3}

p o l o polo polo
_{4   3 3 3}

p o p s pops pops
³
_{4   3 4}

p u p s pups pups
³
_{4   1 4}

p u p a pupa pupa
⁴
_{4   1 4}

LESSON 19

– THE $\boxed{\text{Y}}$ KEY – Right hand 1ˢᵗ finger extension

– *Exercises* –

Practice with Rhythm

₂
y e l l yell yell
1   3 3

y o y o yoyo yoyo
1   3 1   3

y o l k yolk yolk
1   3 3 2

₁
y o u r your your
1   2 1

₂
y o k e yoke yoke
1   3 2

4   3   3
y a w s yaws yaws
1

89

y a r d yard yard
1 4 1 2

y e a r year year
1 2 4 1

y o r e yore yore
1 3 1 2

y u r t yurt yurt
1 1 1 1

y o g a yoga yoga
1 3 1 4

y o w l yowl yowl
1 3 3 3

y o g i yogi yogi
1 3 2 1

y e a h yeah yeah

y e l p yelp yelp

y a p s yaps yaps

Sentences made from Words of Lessons 10-19

– *Exercises* –

Practice Rhythmically

The poor twit quit.

*First read each sentence aloud, and then **rhythmically** type it down once using a period at the end.*

They will prep a tour.

The twit wore a rope.

He will trot to the tree.

Your yoyo is in the yurt.

He got his yoyo on a trip.

He wore a tutu at his rite.

He will tout a type of tree.

The pert boy made a quip.

She wore a tutu and wept.

The peer will weep for the riot.

The pope will tout a type of rite.

The poor peer had to find a euro.

She will type the tort for her peer.

His peer will see a yurt on his tour.

The twit quit when he made a typo.

The peer will use wire to make a weir.

The peer was pert when he got a yoyo.

They tied a rope to the root of the tree.

He got a euro on his trip to see the pope.

Exercises on the 4 punctuations signs located on the Top Row

Square Brackets	**[ ]**
Curly Brackets	**{ }**
Backslash	****
Vertical bar	**|**

Exercises on the Square Brackets [ ]

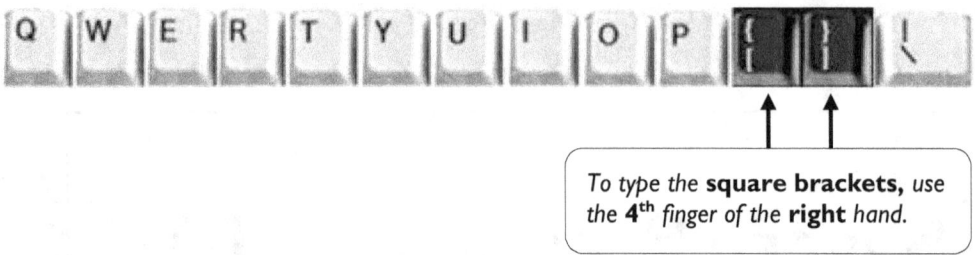

To type the **square brackets,** use the **4**[th] finger of the **right** hand.

– *Exercises* –
Practice with Rhythm

[weir wire wore]

[wept quip quit]

[tort typo tour]

[troy true type]

Exercises on the Curly Brackets { }

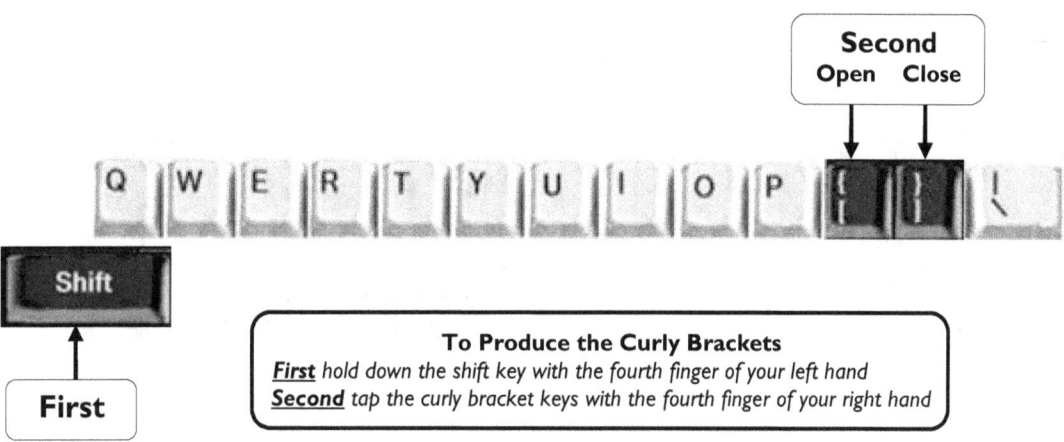

Second
Open Close

Shift

First

To Produce the Curly Brackets
__First__ hold down the shift key with the fourth finger of your left hand
__Second__ tap the curly bracket keys with the fourth finger of your right hand

– *Exercise* –
Practice with Rhythm

{weep root tree}

{toot putt pert}

{yoyo your yore}

Pattern of the keys
*Hold down the shift key – tap the open curly bracket key – Type the three words – hold down the shift key again – tap the close curly bracket key – space. Hit the **enter** key.*

{yurt wert poop}

{poor peer prep}

Exercises on the Backslash \

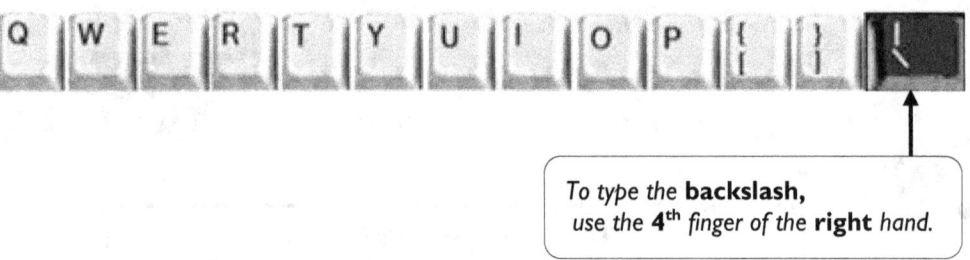

To type the **backslash,**
use the **4**th finger of the **right** hand.

– *Exercises* –
Practice with Rhythm

rite\ rite\

ripe\ ripe\

rope\ rope\

rout\ rout\

repo\ repo\

euro\ euro\

etui\ etu

Exercises on the Vertical Bar |

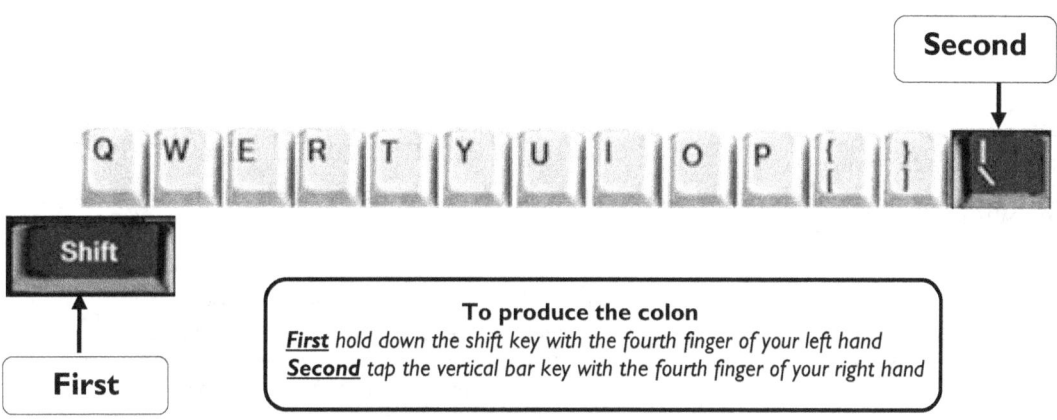

Second

Shift

First

> **To produce the colon**
> ___First___ *hold down the shift key with the fourth finger of your left hand*
> ___Second___ *tap the vertical bar key with the fourth finger of your right hand*

– Exercises –

Practice with Rhythm

were were|

tutu tutu|

tout tout|

> **Pattern of the keys**
> *Type the word twice — hold down the shift key — tap the vertical bar key — space.*
> *Repeat this pattern for each word then hit the* **enter** *key.*

trot trot|

twit twit|

pope pope|

pipe pipe|

LESSON 20

– THE $\boxed{V}$ KEY –

– *Exercises* –

Practice with Rhythm

1 2   2 1
v e e r veer veer

1   1   4
v i v a viva viva
2

1   1   2
v i v e vive vive
2

1 4 3 2
v a s e vase vase

1 4 3 **1**
v a s t vast vast

1 2 3 **1**
v e s t vest vest

Instructions for All the Exercises

> **Pattern of the Exercises**
> *Letter* <u>space</u> *letter* <u>space</u> *letter* <u>space</u> *letter* <u>space</u>
> *Letter letter letter letter* <u>space</u> *letter letter letter letter* <u>space</u>
> Hit the **Enter** key after each line of words

> The exercises are to be typed in **lowercase** *font* **size 20** *on a page set-up in* **print layout view**.

> *When typing the word the* **first** *time, which is spaced-out, look down at the keyboard to memorize the keys; when typing it regularly the* **second** *and* **third** *time, look up at screen to check its spelling.*

> *Before typing each word, say it aloud once, and then type it down three times*

> *After typing 7 or 8 lines of words scroll the page up to keep a comfortable eye-line*

100

1 2 **1** 3
v e t s vets vets

1 4 **1** 3
v a t s vats vats

1 4   3
v a n s vans vans
       1

1 4 1
v a r y vary vary
       1

1 2 1 **1**
v e r b verb verb

1 2 1
v e r y very very
       1

1 2 **1**
v e t o veto veto
       3

1 4
v a i n vain vain
       2 1

1   4
v a m p vamp vamp
1   4

1   2
v e i l veil veil
2   3

1   2
v e i n vein vein
2   1

1   4   2
v a l e vale vale
3

1   4   2
v a n e vane vane
1

1   2   2
v e n d vend vend
1

> Re-type each lesson a few times around

> After typing the last word of a lesson, completely clear
> the pages on the screen for the next round of practice

> **Apply all of the boxed instructions above to all of the 26 lessons**

LESSON 21

– THE $\boxed{C}$ KEY –

– *Exercises* –
Practice with Rhythm

2
c o o l cool cool
  3 3 3

2
c o o k cook cook
  3 3 2

2
c o o p coop coop
  3 3 1

2
c u l l cull cull
  1 3 3

2 4
c a l l call call
  3 3

2 2
c e l l cell cell
  3 3

2   **1**

c o o t coot coot

  3 3

2   1 1

c u f f cuff cuff

 1

2 2 2 2

c e d e cede cede

2   2

c o c o coco coco

  3   3

2 4 2 3

c a d s cads cads

2 4 1 3

c a r s cars cars

2 4 1 2

c a r d card card

2 4 3 2

c a s e case case

2 4 3 2
c a v e cave cave

2 4 3 3
c a w s caws caws

2
c l i p clip clip
3 2 3

2
c l o p clop clop
3 3 4

2
c h i p chip chip
1 3 4

2
c h o p chop chop
1 3 4

LESSON 22

– THE X KEY –

– Exercises –
Practice with Rhythm

4 3 2 3
a x e s axes axes

1 2 3 1
t e x t text text

3 4 3
w a x y waxy waxy
1

1 4 3
t a x i taxi taxi
2

3
o n y x onyx onyx
3 1 1

4 3 3
a x i s axis axis
2

4 3 2

a x l e axle axle

3

2 3 1

e x i t exit exit

2

2 3 1

n e x t next next

1

LESSON 23

– *Exercises* –
Practice with Rhythm

4
z o o m zoom zoom
 3   3   1

4   3
z o o s zoos zoos
 3   3

4 2 2 3
z e d s zeds zeds

4 2 3 **1**
z e s t zest zest

4 2 **1** 4
z e t a zeta zeta

4 2 1
z e r o zero zero
 3

108

4 2 4
z e a l zeal zeal
3

4 2 **1**
z e b u zebu zebu
1

4 4
z a n y zany zant
1 **1**

4 4 3
z a p s zaps zaps
4

4 2
z i n c zinc zinc
2 1

4 3
z i p s zips zips
2 4

4 2
z o n e zone zone
3 1

LESSON 24

– THE B KEY – Left Hand 1st Finger Extension

– *Exercises* –

Practice with Rhythm

1

b o o m boom boom
3 3 1

1

b u l l bull bull
1 3 3

1

b i l l bill bill
2 3 3

1

b o o k book book
3 3 2

1

b o o n boon boon
3 3 1

1 2 2 3

b e e s bees bees

110

¹ ² ² ¹
b e e f beef beef

¹ ² ² ¹
b e e r beer beer

¹ ² ² ¹
b e e t beet beet

¹ ⁴
b a l l ball ball
    ₃ ₃

¹ ⁴ ³ ³
b a s s bass bass

¹   ³ ³
b o s s boss boss
 ₃

¹   ¹
b o o r boor boor
 ₃   ₃

¹   ¹
b o o t boot boot
 ₃   ₃

1   3

b o o s boos boos

  3 3

1 2 2

b e e n been been

      1

1 2 2

b e e p beep beep

      4

1   1 1

b u f f buff buff

  1

1   4 4

b u z z buzz buzz

  1

1 2

b e l l bell bell

  3 3

LESSON 25

– *Exercises* –
Practice with Rhythm

n o o n noon noon
1 3 3 1

n o o k nook nook
1 3 3 2

1 1 3 3
n u l l null null

2 2 2
n e e d need need
1

2
n i n e nine nine
1 2 1

2
n o n e none none
1 3 1

113

[3]

n u n s nuns nuns

[1] [1] [1]

[2]

n e o n neon neon

[1] [3] [1]

[2] [3] [3]

n e w s news news

[1]

[2] [1] [2]

n e r d nerd nerd

[1]

[2] [4] [1]

n e a r near near

[1]

[2] [1] [3]

n e t s nets nets

[1]

[2] [4] [1]

n e a t neat neat

[1]

[2] [3] [1]

n e s t nest nest

[1]

n e x t next next
[2] [3] [1]
[1]

n e w t newt newt
[2] [3] [1]
[1]

n i p s nips nips
[3]
[1] [2] [4]

n u k e nuke nuke
[2]
[1] [1] [2]

n o s e nose nose
[3] [2]
[1] [3]

n o d s nods nods
[2] [3]
[1] [3]

LESSON 26

– *Exercises* –

Practice with Rhythm

m i l l mill mill
1 2 3 3

m o o n moon moon
1   3   3   1

m u l l mull mull
1   1 3 3

m o l l moll moll
1   3 3 3

      2
m o o d mood mood
1   3 3

     1
m o o r moor moor
1   3 3

        2 2 **1**
m e e t meet meet
1

        3 3
m i s s miss miss
1   2

        1 1
m i t t mitt mitt
1   2

        3 3
m o s s moss moss
1   3

        3 3
m u s s muss muss
1   1

        2 2
m e e k meek meek
1   2

        4
m a l l mall mall
1   3 3

m i n k mink mink
1   2   1 2

m i n i mini mini
1　2　1　2

4　2　2
m a d e made made
1

4　1　2
m a r e mare mare
1

2　4　2
m e a d mead mead
1

3　2
m u s e muse muse
1　1

1　2
m u t e mute mute
1　1

Sentences made from Words of Lessons 20-26

– *Exercises* –

Practice Rhythmically

The vats had a chip.

> First read each sentence aloud, and then **rhythmically** type it down once using a period at the end.

Cars vary from vans.

The cads chip the cars.

The card was in the case.

They made a vase to vend.

The cads will chop the bass.

He zips the case of the chip.

The ball at the mall will vary.

The vast vats are in the mall.

She will vend a chip in the mall.

He will eat the chip in the mall.

She will call the cads to the vale.

They will put the ball in the case.

They made a case with the cads.

The cads will clip and chip the cars.

The set of cards will vary in each case.

He will buy a ball and a card in the mall.

He will vend a vase from one of his vans.

She will use her card to buy a vase at the mall.

They will know how to use a vast set of caws.

Exercises on the 5 punctuations signs located on the Bottom Row

Comma	**,**
Period	**.**
Pointed Brackets	**< >**
Slash	**/**
Question mark	**?**

Exercises on the Comma ,

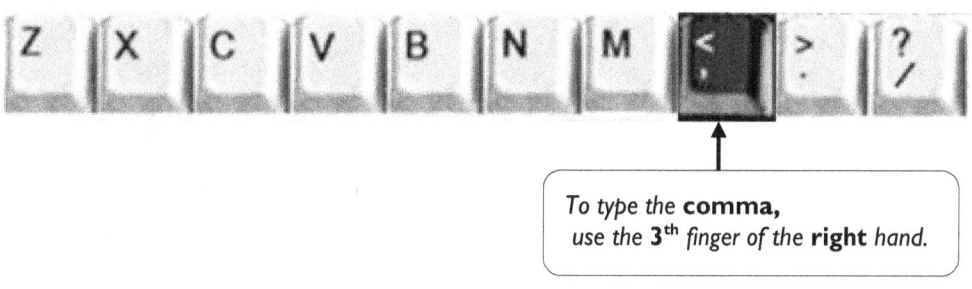

To type the **comma,**
use the **3**th finger of the **right** hand.

– *Exercises* –
Practice with Rhythm

call, call,

bass, bass,

ball, ball,

mall, mall,

cads, cads,

Exercises on the Period .

To type the **period,**
use the **4**th finger of the **right** hand.

– *Exercises* –
Practice with Rhythm

call. call.

bass. bass.

ball. ball.

mall. mall.

cads. cads.

Exercises on the Pointed Brackets < >

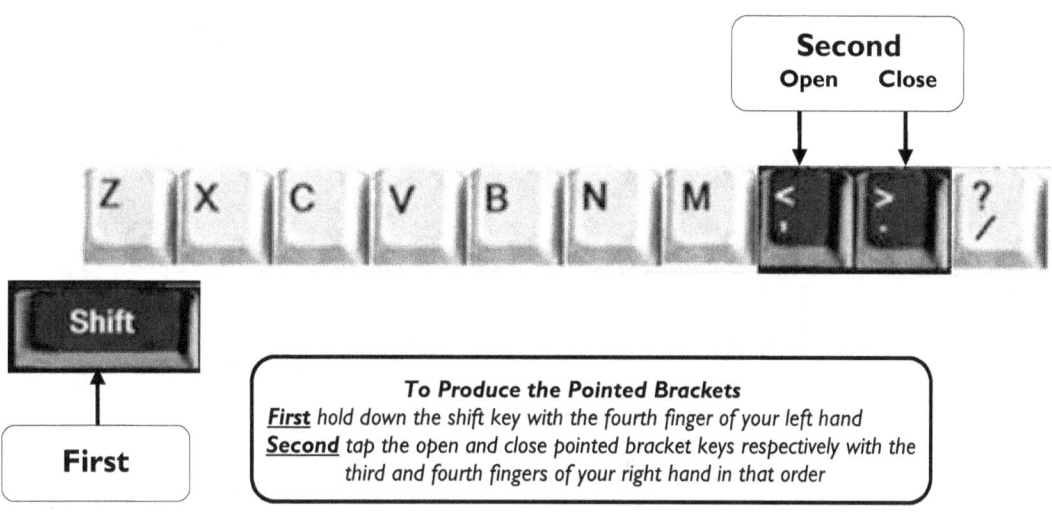

Second
Open   Close

First

To Produce the Pointed Brackets
First hold down the shift key with the fourth finger of your left hand
Second tap the open and close pointed bracket keys respectively with the third and fourth fingers of your right hand in that order

– Exercises –
Practice with Rhythm

<call bass ball mall cads>

<call bass ball mall cads>

Pattern of the keys
Hold down the shift key – tap the open pointed bracket key – Type the five words – hold down the shift key again – tap the close pointed bracket key – space.
*Hit the **enter** key.*

Exercises on the Slash /

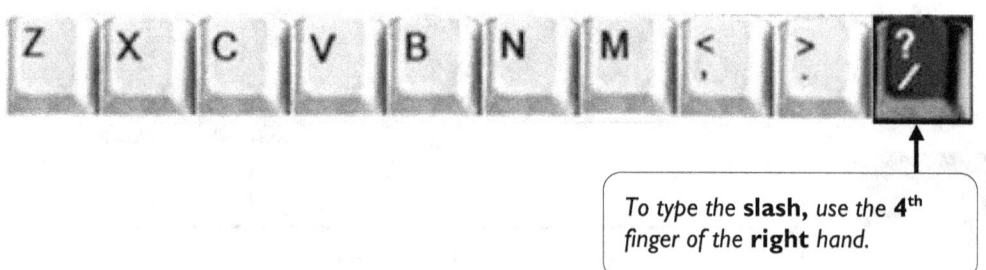

To type the **slash**, *use the* **4**th *finger of the* **right** *hand.*

– *Exercises* –
Practice with Rhythm

call/ call/

bass/ bass/

ball/ ball/

mall/ mall/

cads/ cads/

126

Exercises on the Question Mark ?

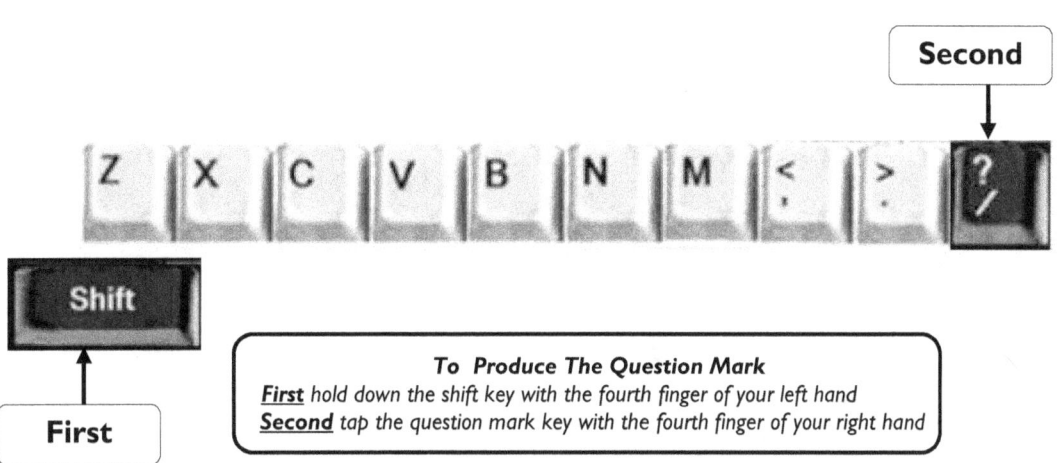

Second

First

To Produce The Question Mark
First hold down the shift key with the fourth finger of your left hand
Second tap the question mark key with the fourth finger of your right hand

– *Exercises* –
Practice with Rhythm

call call?

bass bass?

Pattern of the keys
Type the word twice – hold down the shift key – tap the question mark key – space.
Repeat this pattern for each word then hit the **enter** *key.*

ball ball?

mall mall?

cads cads?

Other Signs and Symbols

Left Hand Fingering

| 4 | 3 | 2 | 1 | **1** | | | | | |

1 1 2 3 4

Right Hand Fingering

!	Exclamation Point
@	At
#	Number or Pound
$	Dollars
%	Percent
&	Ampersand
*	Asterisk or Star
( )	Parenthesis
–	Hyphen – Dash – Minus
_	Underscore
=	Equal
+	Plus

Exclamation Point

The **!** sign is used after a sentence that externalize emotions such as surprise, sensation, outcry, happiness etc. To emphasize or amplify further the above emotions, the exclamation point can be doubled or tripled. Do not space in-between a word and an exclamation point.

Examples :

> → *WOW!*
> → *Help!!*
> → *Happy Birthday!!!*

To produce the !

- *First*, Press and hold down the right side **Shift-key** with the pinky of your right hand;
- *Second*, With the pinky of your left hand, tap the key where there is the **number 1**, it will now produce the **!**

At

The @ symbol is used to substitute the words "*at*" and "*at a rate of*" mostly in numerical business accounting; in this case @ is usually typed among words or numbers with one space before and one after. Also, @ is the symbol used in computer e-mail addresses, in this case there are no spaces before or after it.

Examples :

→   *I bought 50 boxes of apples @ $20 a box.*
→   *jdoe@trade.com*

To produce the @

- *First,* Press and hold down the right side **Shift-key** with the pinky of your right hand;
- *Second,* With your third finger of your left hand tap the key where there is the **number 2**, it will now produce the @

Number or Pound

The **#** symbol is used to abbreviate the word **"number"**, and the word **"pounds"** as a unit of weight. When the **#** follows a number it is to be read as *pounds*; when it precedes a number it is to be read as *number*. Do not space between the **#** and the corresponding number.

Examples :

- ➔ *No. 3   or   #3*
- ➔ *50 lbs   or   50#*

To Produce the # :

- *First*, Press and hold down the right side **Shift-key** with the pinky of your right hand;
- *Second*, With your second finger of your left hand tap the key where there is the **number 3**, it will now produce **#**

Dollar

The **$** symbol is used to indicate that the number that follows is an amount of money in dollars. Do not space between the **$** and the corresponding amount of money.

Examples :

→ *$1 $10 $125*
→ *$.99 (ninety-nine cents of a dollar)*
→ *$.50 (fifty cents of a dollar)*
→ *$.04 (four cents of a dollar)*

To produce the $

- *First*, Press and hold down the right side **Shift-key** with the pinky of your right hand;
- *Second*, With your first finger of your left hand tap the key where there is the **number 4**, it will now produce **$**

Percent

The % symbol is used as a way of expressing a proportion or a fraction in relation to a whole. Do not space between the number and the % .

Examples :

→   1%   5%   14%   100%

To produce the %

- *First*, Press and hold down the right side **Shift-key** with the pinky of your right hand;
- *Second*, With your first finger of your left hand tap the key where there is the **number 5**, it will now produce %

Ampersand

The **&** symbol is used to substitute the conjunction "*and*" between two names associated as a business entity; and between two proper names and formal titles. In screenplays the **&** symbol indicates a closer partnership than the word "and".

Examples :

→ *Smith & Benson*
→ *Lee & sons*
→ *The U.S.A. & Protector of Guam*
→ *David Spielberg & Tom Coppola*

To produce the &

- *First,* Press and hold down the left side **Shift-key** with the pinky of your left hand;
- *Second,* With your first finger of your right hand tap the key where there is the **number** *7*, it will now produce **&**

Asterisk or Star

The * symbol is used as **_footnote_*** mark on particular words in a text which directs you to additional explanations about those words at the bottom of the page; as a multiplication sign while using the keyboard; and to put before and after words to emphasize them. Do not space between words and the * ; when the * is used as a multiplication sign type one space before and one after it.

Examples :

➜ **_footnote_***   *to mention as a source.*

➜ *3 * 3 = 9*

To produce the *

- *First*, Press and hold down the left side **Shift-key** with the pinky of your left hand;
- *Second*, with your second right finger tap the key where there is the **number 8**, it will now produce the *

Parenthesis

The **( )** signs are used to include explanatory remarks, comments or notes in the middle of a sentence; to mark off a joint article in a mathematical operation; and after a number or letter to list points etc. Do not space between the **( )** and the first and last word or number contained in them.

Examples :

➔   *…..she was wearing that blouse (the beige one in silk) …..*
➔   *5 + 2 (4 + x)*
➔   *1) 2) 3) 4) 5) etc.*

To produce the ( )

- *First*, Press and hold down the left side **Shift-key** with the pinky of your left hand;
- *Second*, with your third right finger tap the key where there is the **number 9**, it will now produce the **(**
- *Third*, Press and hold down the left side **Shift-key** with the pinky of your left hand
- *Fourth*, with your fourth right finger tap the key where there is the **number 0 (zero)** which will now produce the **)**

Hyphen - Dash - Minus

The — symbol is used between the segment of a compound word or name; between the syllables of a word; to replace a comma or parenthesis between words; and as a subtraction sign used for mathematical purposes.

As Hyphen, is used between the two segments of a compound word or name. Do not space before or after this sign.

Examples :

➜   _Look-out_
➜   _in-law_

As Dash, between words when replacing a comma or parenthesis. Do not space between the — and the first and last word or number contained in them.

Examples :

➜   _Just two people in class were absent —Bob_
       and Jim— everyone else was present.

As Minus, a subtraction sign used for mathematical purposes. Before and after the minus sign type one space.

Examples :

→   _4 – 3 = 1_

To produce the –

- With your fourth finger of your right hand tap the key on the right of the **number _0_** key which will produce –

Underscore

The _ is used to make form lines meant to be filled out, such as in: a job application, a doctor file, a contract form, etc. It is also used to replace spacing in e-mail addresses.

Underscore cannot be used to underline.

(To <u>underline</u> words, use the <u>U</u> in the window's formatting toolbar, right above the document you are typing on.)

Examples :

➔ *Name: First_____Mid_____Last_____*

➔ *tim_smith@abc.com*

To produce the _

- *First*, Press and hold down with your left hand's pinky the left side **Shift-key**;
- *Second*, With your fourth finger of your right hand tap the key where there is the **– (dash)** , it will now produce _

Equal

The **=** is used for accounting matters or can be used to fill in empty spaces in legal documents (such as a will or a contract) in order to seal the original text content so that no other words can be later added to fraudulently change that document.

Examples :

➜   *3 – 2 =1*

➜   *I, Tom Mann declare that all my personal belongings, and all the deposits of my bank accounts and safe deposit box goes to my sister, Ester Mann.===============*

To produce the =

- With your fourth right finger simply tap the key where there is the **+ *(plus)*,** it will now produce the **=**

Plus

The **+** sign is used mostly for math purposes to indicate addition or a positive quantity. Type one space before and one after the **+** .

Examples :

➔   *2 + 2*
➔   *12 + 24*
➔   *100 + 200*

To produce the +

- *First*, Press and hold down the left side **Shift-key** with the pinky of your left hand;
- *Second*, with your fourth right finger of your right hand tap the key where there is the **= (equal)**, it will now produce the **+**

Table of
Roman Numerals

All the Roman Numbers can be graphically made with the use of only 7 letters of the alphabet in uppercase: I, V, X, L, C, D, M. Roman numerals do not include the number zero.

$$I \ = \ 1$$

$$V \ = \ 5$$

$$X \ = \ 10$$

$$L \ = \ 50$$

$$C \ = \ 100$$

$$D \ = \ 500$$

$$M \ = \ 1000$$

The combination of any of the above numbers will make any other needed number.

II = 2	III = 3	IV = 4	VI = 6
VII = 7	VIII = 8	IX = 9	XI = 11
XV = 15	XXV = 25	XXXV = 35	LX = 60

A bigger number in front of a smaller number equals the sum of both numbers.

$$V + I = VI \quad \rightarrow \quad 5 + 1 = 6$$
$$X + I = XI \quad \rightarrow \quad 10 + 1 = 11$$
$$L + I = LI \quad \rightarrow \quad 50 + 1 = 51$$
$$L + V = LV \quad \rightarrow \quad 50 + 5 = 55$$

A smaller number in front of a bigger number equals the difference of the bigger number and the smaller number.

$$V - I = IV \quad \rightarrow \quad 5 - 1 = 4$$
$$X - I = IX \quad \rightarrow \quad 10 - 1 = 9$$
$$L - V = VL \quad \rightarrow \quad 50 - 5 = 45$$
$$L - X = XL \quad \rightarrow \quad 50 - 10 = 40$$
$$C - L = LC \quad \rightarrow \quad 100 - 50 = 50$$
$$C - X = XC \quad \rightarrow \quad 100 - 10 = 90$$

Two equal numbers equal the sum of both Numbers.

$$X + X = XX \quad \rightarrow \quad 10 + 10 = 20$$
$$C + C = CC \quad \rightarrow \quad 100 + 100 = 200$$
$$M + M = MM \quad \rightarrow \quad 1000 + 1000 = 2000$$

Brief History of The Typewriter

No one person can be said to have invented the typewriter, like Edison invented the light bulb, like Marconi invented the telegraph, and like Alexander Graham Bell invented the telephone.

The roots of the idea of a typewriter are to be found in the concept of movable type developed by Johan Guttenberg in the invention of the printing press.

The first known man to whom was granted for the first time a patent for a machine that, by its description on records, sounds similar to a typewriter was Henry Mill, an Englishman, in 1714. It was not sure whether the machine was actually built or produced but the idea was there; anyway, the first step on the way to building a typing machine at an affordable price that writes faster than the hand had began.

In 1808, **Pelligrino Turri** further developed a typing machine and also invented and introduced the use of carbon paper. Besides finding a fast way to write, the designs of these early machines were also intended to allow the blind to write.

In 1829 **William Austin Burt** patented a machine called the *Typographer* (Picture 1), like many of these early machines; it is sometimes listed as the first typewriter. The science museum in London describes it merely as the first writing mechanism whose invention was documented.

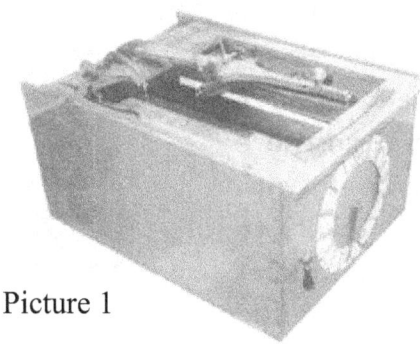

Typographer

Picture 1

The Hanson Writing Ball

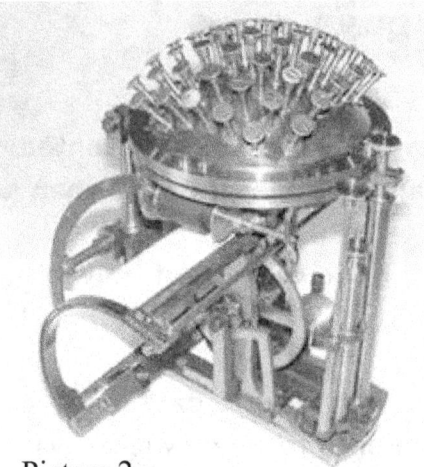

Picture 2

From 1829 to 1830, many printing or typing machines were patented by inventors in America and Europe, but none went into commercial production.

In 1865 reverend Malling Hanson from Denmark, teacher and director of an institution for the deaf and dumb, invented *The Hanson writing ball* (Picture 2), a machine aimed to enable his pupils to speak with their fingers. It went into production in 1870 and was the first commercially sold typewriter in Europe.

Malling reasoned that a ball-shaped arrangement of keys would allow touch-typing. Although a considerable number of Hanson's writing balls were produced and sold, its success was limited as the typist operating this machine still could not supersede the speed of hand-writing. The Hanson writing ball had 52 keys, one set of the alphabet in capital and one set in lower case. This machine did not have the shift-key (the shift key was not invented until 1878).

In 1867 Christopher Sholes, Carlos Glidden, and Samuel W. Soule from Milwaukee, Wisconsin invented a typewriter and they patented what was to be the first useful typewriter. The Sholes and Glidden typewriter was the first typing device that finally would allow an operator to type substantially faster than a person could write by hand.

The patent drawing for the Sholes and Glidden typewriter was sold for $12,000 to Densmore and Yost who made an agreement with Remington & Sons (the noted gun maker) to commercialize what was known as the Sholes and Glidden typewriter. Remington started the

Remington Model 1

Picture 3

production of their first typewriter in the fall of 1873 and by the early 1874 the first models appeared on the market under the name of *Remington Model 1* (Picture 3).

Remington Model 2

Picture 4

In 1878 **Sholes, Glidden, and Soule, while always being in cooperation with the Remington Industry to improve further the** *Sholes and Glidden* **typewriter commercially called** *Remington Model 1*, **rearranged the layout of the letter keys by setting apart the most often used letters so that the corresponding type bars of those most used letters would not jam when being typed quickly and consecutively, this new keyboard layout was introduced as the QWERTY layout which refers to the 6 letter keys of the left part of the top row on any standard keyboard which was later introduced on the** *Remington Model 2* (Picture 4) **which went in production that very same year.**

In the next fifty years other modifications and improvements were made to the typewriter; by the 1920's virtually all typewriters were look a likes: front stroke, QWERTY key board layout, type bar machines, printing through a ribbon, using one shift key and four banks (rows) of keys.

IBM Selectric

In regard to the electric typewriter, it must be said that even though the first rudimental electric typewriter was invented back in 1872 by Thomas Edison it did not become of widespread common use until the 1950's.

IBM and Remington electric typewriters were the leading competitors until 1961

Picture 5

when **IBM** introduced the very innovative, groundbreaking *IBM Selectric Typewriter* (Picture 5), **which replaced the type bars with a spherical type ball, slightly smaller than a golf ball with the letters molded on its surface. The basic spherical type ball on the typewriter could be easily manually removed and interchanged with other additional type balls that have different font styles of letters molded on their surface** (Picture 6) **so to allow the typing of different variety of letter styles.**

The *IBM Selectric* typewriter occasionally known as the *IBM golf ball typewriter* is the electric typewriter design that brought the typewriter into the electric age and is generally considered to be a designed classic.

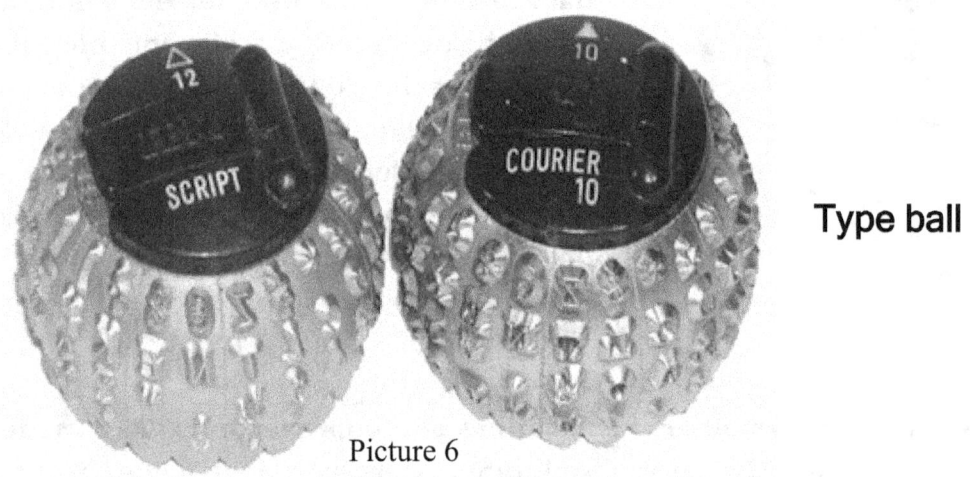

Type ball

Picture 6

The latest major development of the typewriter is the *electronic typewriter*. Most electronic typewriters replace the **IBM** type ball with the *Daisy Wheel* mechanism (Picture 7) **which is a disc with the letters molded on the outside edge of its "petals". A plastic** *Daisy Wheel* **is much simpler and cheaper than a type ball but wears out more easily. Some electronic typewriters are dedicated word processors with internal memory and cartridges or diskette external memory storage devices. Unlike the Selectrics and earlier models, these really are electronic and rely on integrated circuits and multiple electromechanical components.**

Daisy Wheel

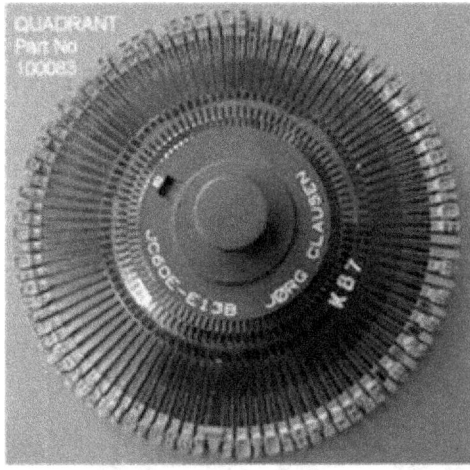

Picture 7

The electronic typewriters (a typewriter with an electronic memory capable of storing text) first appeared in 1978, they were developed independently by the Olivetti co. in Italy and the Casio co. in Japan. (Picture 8)

Adler-Royal / Olivetti Satellite 80 - Premium Electronic Typewriter

Picture 8

The electric typewriter is the immediate precursor of the computer keyboard in use nowadays. (Picture 9)

Logitech Deluxe Access Keyboard

Picture 9